Zero Gravity

Sarah Fleming

Contents

A Gravity Experiment

Take two books...
one on Earth...
and one in space.
Drop them both.

This one falls.
Why?

This book is on Earth.
Earth's force of
gravity pulls it down.

This one doesn't
fall. Why?
This book is in a
spaceship. There is
almost no gravity here.

Gravity and Zero Gravity

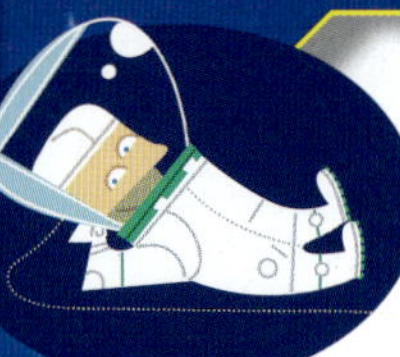

More than 300 years ago, Newton saw an apple fall. He called the force that pulled the apple *gravity*.

Gravity is the force that pulls things toward something very, very large – like a planet.

Newton figured out that there was a force pulling things to the center of the Earth.

Gravity in a spaceship flying around the Earth is only one millionth of the gravity on Earth. That's $\frac{1}{1,000,000}$!

The force of gravity in a spaceship is so weak it is called **microgravity**. Microgravity is so small, it is often called **zero gravity**.

What would be easier or more difficult for a person to do in space? Think about jumping, writing, lifting things, sleeping, etc.

Zero Gravity and a Body

When a person goes into space, zero gravity feels strange at first. The person feels dizzy and doesn't know which way is up.

Astronauts get space sickness, which is kind of like feeling car sick. It usually goes away after about three days.

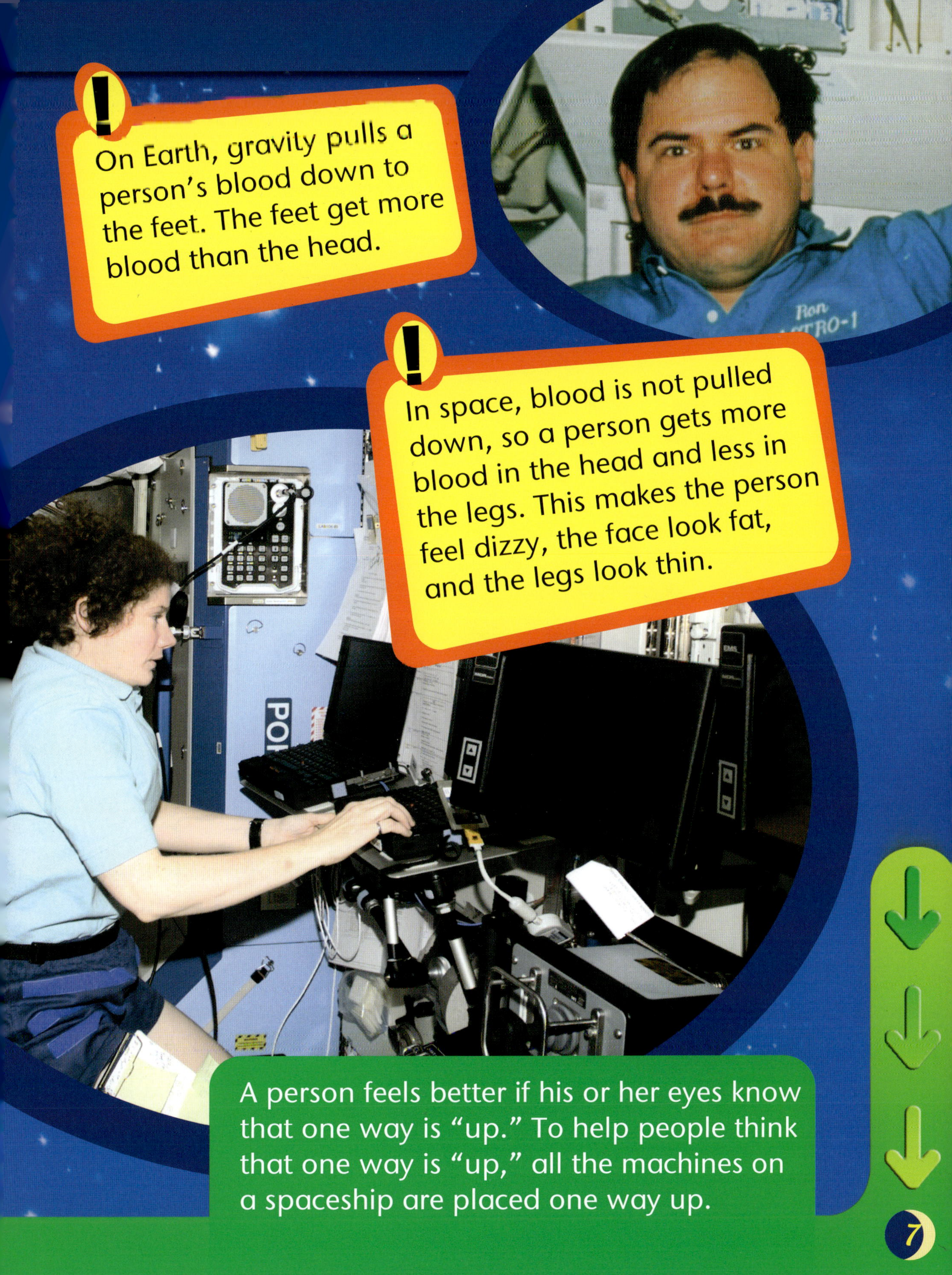

On Earth, gravity pulls a person's blood down to the feet. The feet get more blood than the head.

In space, blood is not pulled down, so a person gets more blood in the head and less in the legs. This makes the person feel dizzy, the face look fat, and the legs look thin.

A person feels better if his or her eyes know that one way is "up." To help people think that one way is "up," all the machines on a spaceship are placed one way up.

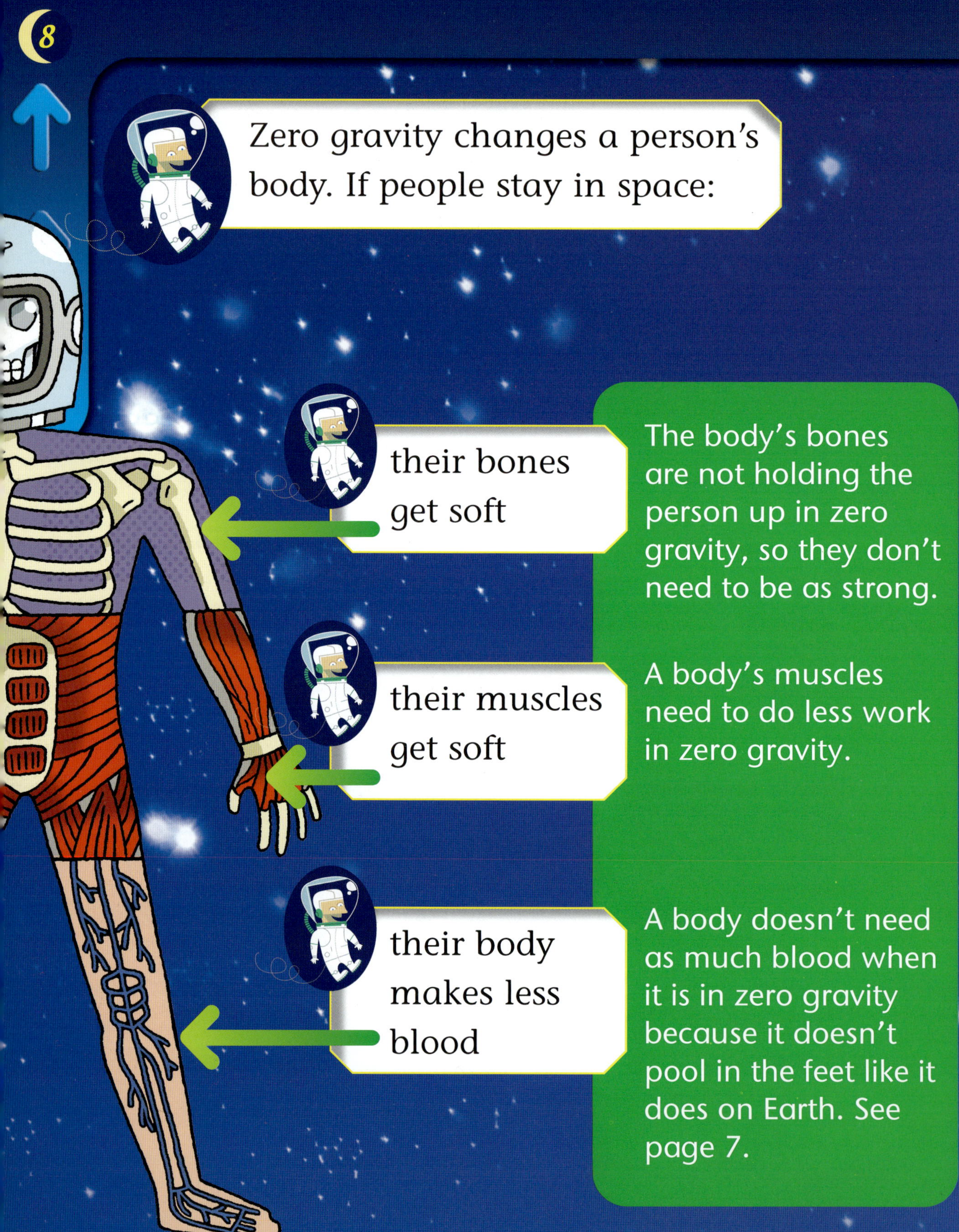

The body's bones are not holding the person up in zero gravity, so they don't need to be as strong.

A body's muscles need to do less work in zero gravity.

A body doesn't need as much blood when it is in zero gravity because it doesn't pool in the feet like it does on Earth. See page 7.

People need to stay in shape in space.

There are many ways of staying in shape in space.

When the person gets back to Earth, the body will make more blood again...

There are special exercises to make the bones strong.

...and the person will have to work to get the bones and muscles strong again.

Making Gravity on a Spaceship

On a spaceship, people can use **suction** (like a vacuum cleaner) to make a pulling force like gravity. This can help the person to:

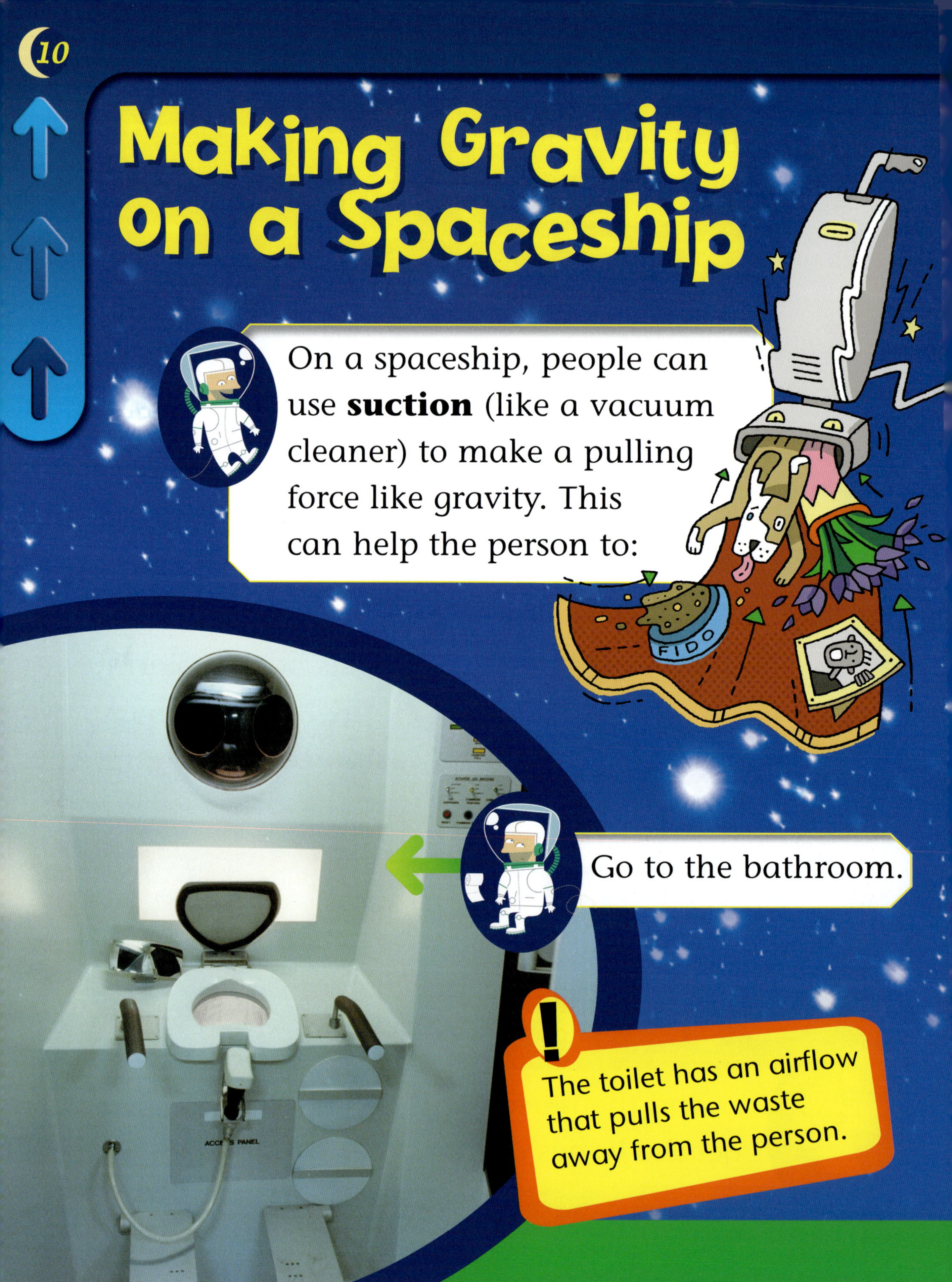

Go to the bathroom.

!

The toilet has an airflow that pulls the waste away from the person.

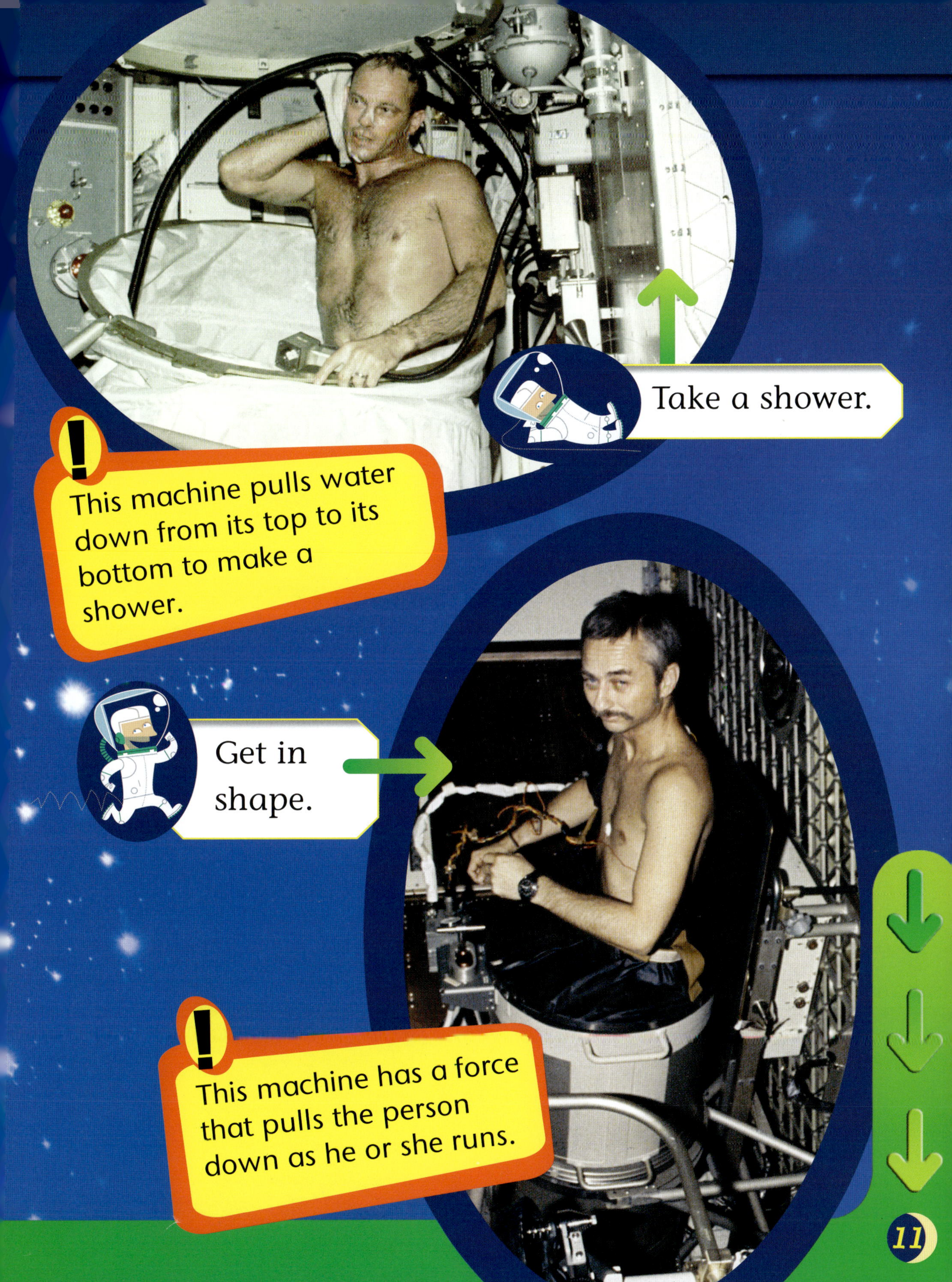
Take a shower.
This machine pulls water down from its top to its bottom to make a shower.
Get in shape.
This machine has a force that pulls the person down as he or she runs.

Other Effects of Zero Gravity

Astronauts can do lots of **experiments** in zero gravity.

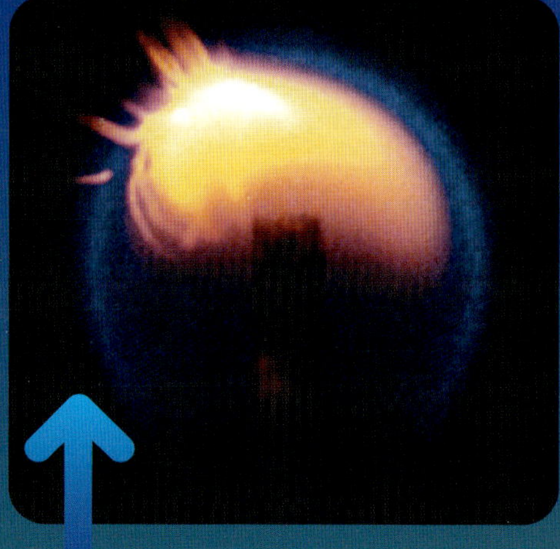

Compare this flame in zero gravity, with this flame on Earth.

What is different?

Look at the way the water boils in zero gravity and on Earth.

What is different?

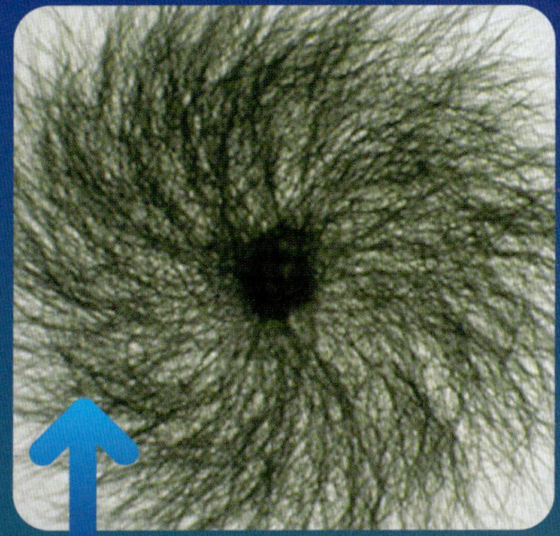

Compare the way plants grow in zero gravity and on Earth.

What is different?

Look Back

1 How long have people known about the force called gravity?

2 What is microgravity?

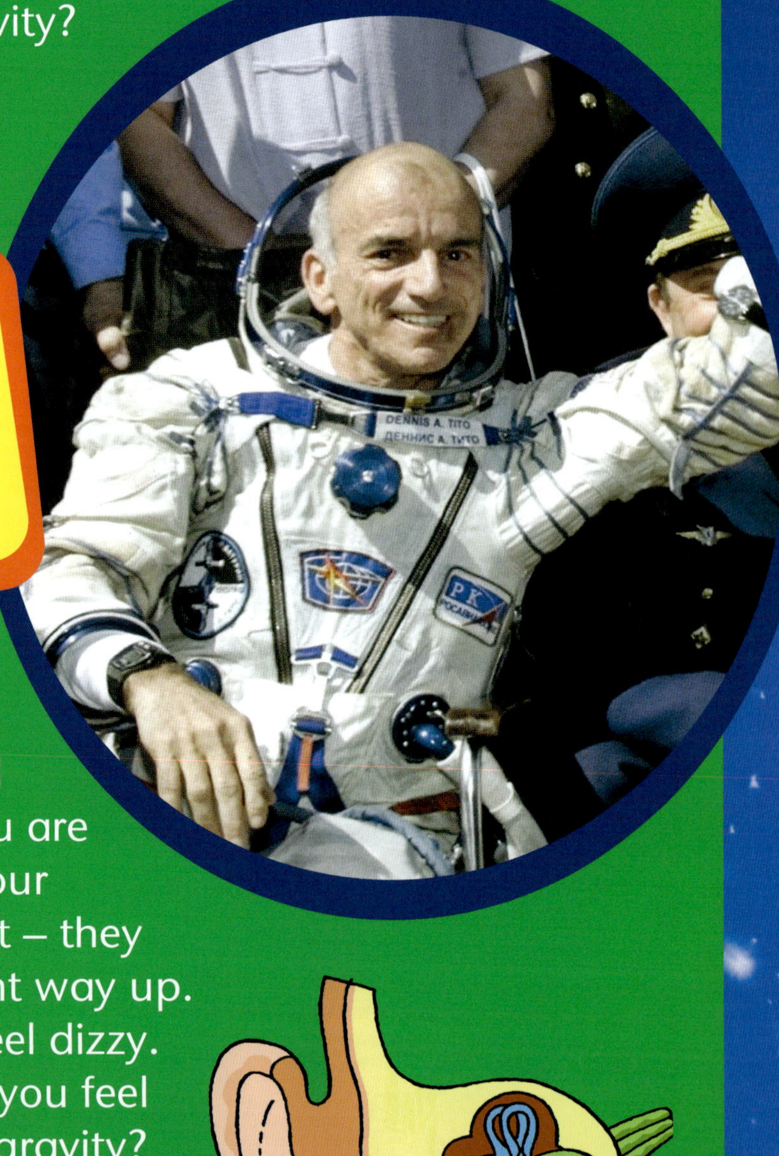

This is Dennis Tito. He was a space tourist. Why do you think he is coming away from the spaceship in a wheelchair?

3 Your ears can feel gravity. When you are in zero gravity, your inner ears feel lost – they can't find the right way up. This makes you feel dizzy. What else makes you feel dizzy about zero gravity?

4 How can suction help you on a spaceship?

Index

Glossary

astronaut – someone who goes into space in a spaceship

experiment – a test made to study what happens to something

gravity – the force that pulls something toward something else that is very big, such as a planet

microgravity – gravity that is very weak, for example in a spaceship traveling around the Earth

suction – a force that pulls things in

zero gravity – a lack of gravity, also another name for microgravity